Published in the United States in 1987 by
Franklin Watts, 387 Park Avenue South, New York, NY10016

© Aladdin Books Ltd

Designed and produced by
Aladdin Books Ltd, 70 Old Compton Street, London W1

ISBN 0 531 17070 5
Library of Congress
Catalog Card No 87 80452

Printed in Belgium

First timers

MOVING HOUSE

KATE PETTY
and
LISA KOPPER

Franklin Watts
New York · London · Toronto · Sydney

There's a big sign outside the house
where Sam and Jenny live.
It says "For Sale." Some people come
to see the house. They may want to buy it.

Sam and Jenny follow Mom
as she shows the visitors around.
They like Sam's room – but so does Sam!
He doesn't want strangers sleeping there.

Mom and Dad have found a new house.
They take Sam and Jenny to see it.
There's an upstairs and a downstairs
and a yard in the back.

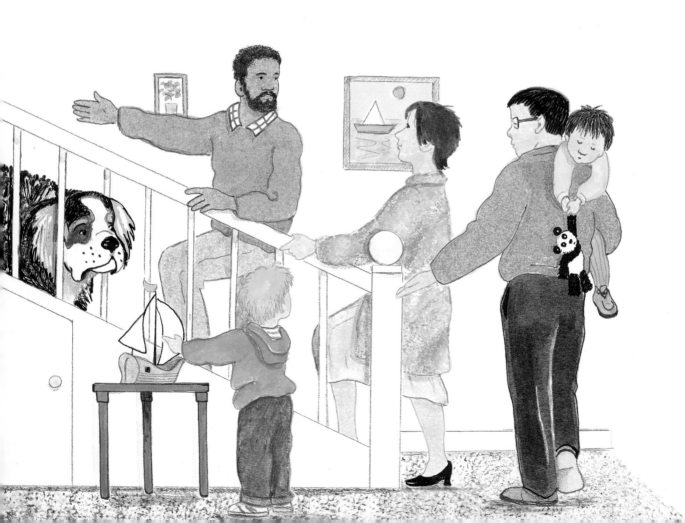

Outside in the yard Jenny has
found a big, friendly dog.
Can they keep him? No, they can't.
Its owners will take the dog with them.

Sam has almost forgotten about moving
but this morning a letter arrives.
"We're going to move in three weeks!"
Sam isn't so happy. He likes his home.

"Will Puss come with us?" asks Jenny.
"Of course," says Mom, "she's ours."
Sam wonders about the new yard
Surely nobody can take that with them!

Now the whole family is very busy.
Everything has to be packed in boxes.
Mom wraps the precious things carefully
so they won't get broken.

The house begins to look very bare
and not like home any more.
Sam thinks perhaps he won't be sorry
to move to the new house.

Today is moving day. A huge van arrives.
The men start to carry out the furniture.
Sam wonders how they can lift it.
Back and forth, in and out they go.

At last everything's neatly packed away.
It's time to follow the van
to the new house. The cat is packed too —
she's safely in her basket. Off they go.

"Here we are. Now we can move in.
Don't let Puss out, Jenny," says Mom.
Sam can't wait to get inside
and explore the empty rooms.

The movers start unloading.
In and out of the house they go again.
Sam rushes out to meet the neighbors.
Jenny will have to meet them tomorrow.

At last the van is empty.
The men all say goodbye.
The kitchen things are still packed,
so Dad goes out to get food for dinner.

Jenny wonders where the cat is.
She's safe and sound, but unhappy.
She needs some food too.

Sam goes upstairs to his very own room.
Jenny's fast asleep already.
Dad takes her up to bed.

She's sleeping alone tonight
so Dad leaves the door ajar.
Dad has promised to paint Sam's room.
Sam wonders what colors to choose.

Now Sam has gone to sleep as well.
Mom and Dad keep working downstairs.
One by one the boxes are unpacked
and the house begins to look like home.

Puss sniffs and prowls about.
But when Mom and Dad sit down
she settles in between them on the sofa.
She will explore the yard tomorrow.

For Sale sign

packing

moving van

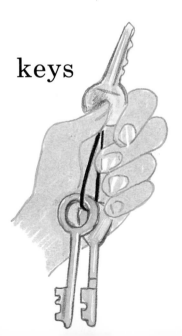

keys

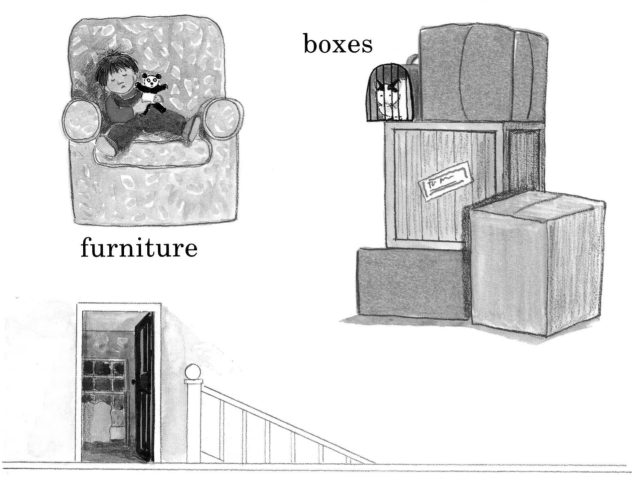

furniture

boxes

upstairs

downstairs

97   9